Meltdown *in* *Paradise*

Marisa De Maio

authorHOUSE®

AuthorHouse™
1663 Liberty Drive
Bloomington, IN 47403
www.authorhouse.com
Phone: 1 (800) 839-8640

Published by AuthorHouse   03/19/2016

ISBN: 978-1-5049-8336-5 (sc)
ISBN: 978-1-5049-8335-8 (e)

Library of Congress Control Number: 2016903554

Print information available on the last page.

You were my one-way ticket to
a meltdown in paradise.

For the recovering heartbroken,
For those who inspired these words—may
you forever remain unknown,
And, most importantly,
For my mother,
Thank you for everything.

Please know that I have been broken and burned so many times, and the only thing that has brought me back on track after every downfall is writing.
It just has this way of healing my soul and bringing me back to life.

I write in order to survive.

Contents

Introduction

I encourage you to keep an open mind as you read the words left on these pages.

Every single last one of these words stems from pain, loss, love, and heartbreak. But just know that after every defeat, I have learned to live again.

I have a strong tendency to see things for what I *want* them to be, instead of what they actually are.

Some of these letters are just pure exaggerations of real-life events that have occurred, but have been altered through my imagination.

Some are dreams that jolted me out of my sleep.

Some are events that have been passed down to me by loved ones. Some of these experiences broke my heart and pained me beyond recognition. With that pain, I did all I knew to release it: write.

Other experiences have been memorized vividly, with every detail an exact replica of the life I have lived—moments that have meant something to me, as well as moments that will leave their mark on my heart for lifetimes to come.

It's ironic actually; the people in my life will swear to you that I do not know love. They will insist that I have never felt it—I never held it in my hand, that I have never experienced it in any human form. Yet, each of these pieces were written straight from a hole in my heart that has yet to be closed, and quite frankly, I don't know ever will be.

Life is all about growing, feeling, learning, and changing.

These pieces are all little fragments of suppressed feelings I have hidden, and been too afraid to face, and to show a single soul,

Until now.

There is such an importance in words, and I now take a comfort in sharing myself through my writing. Writing has healed me every single time destruction entered into my world. Writing is my safe haven, my escape from reality.

I believe God brings certain people into our lives strictly for our own lessons and pure inspiration, in order to better us for our future, and that knowledge has somehow healed me for the simple fact that the brokenness I have felt was for a reason. That reason being for my own lessons that I now will pass on to you.

I have found inspiration within the least deserving of places.

I hope my story is able to strike a chord within your soul. I pray that it inspires you to explore your own heart.

This came from my soul to enter into yours.

Find the words you are too afraid to say. I pray that once you find these words, you have the courage to say them. Say them out loud, say them again before it is too late; say them while you still have the time to do so.

Please know that every single word on these pages, whether truth or fabrication, stemmed from a place of pure honesty that my heart was feeling.

So this is my gift to you—

I hope you enjoy,

learn,

heal,

and love.

I hope your heart feels something as you read the words I have written to you.

And the way I ran from love,
You would have thought I was running for my life.

I swear I thought love was going to kill me.

He Found Me

He found me as the spring rain helped bring to life the season's flowers, and as they bloomed, so did we, together.

I was his, just as the crisp spring air was taken over by the summer heat.
He had me all throughout the summer's sun,
Held me until the moon would appear,
Kissed me under the stars as they shed their light.

He loved me deeper as the leaves changed color,
Kissed my lips, cheeks, and neck whenever he could, and he didn't care who was watching.
He wanted the world to know that I belonged to him.
But as the leaves started to fall to the ground, something started to die.

As winter crept in, the warmth of his touch started to turn cold.
I don't know if it was the ice that stole the fire from his heart, or if his heart was always cold to begin with, and I had only been blinded.
But as the snow started to melt and spring was about to appear again, as quickly as the seasons changed, so did he.
This time, he was gone before the flowers bloomed.

Haunted

I am haunted by both the words I was too afraid to speak—
Words the universe will never know—
As well as the cruelty I blurted out through brokenness that
will forever be etched into existence.

Good Girls

He said, "Good girls don't wear thigh-highs and mini skirts."
While taking a long drag from his cigarette,
His eyes fixated on mine.

I smiled.
"Well, if that's the case, darling, then you're staring at a living contradiction."

Living Contradiction

He was a living contradiction in every sense of the phrase—

He made it easy to hate him,
Yet even easier to love him.

He was arrogant,
Yet humble.
Charismatic,
Yet shy.
He wanted to settle down,
But his heart lived in disorder.

He craved change,
Yet continued to stand stagnant.

He wanted a good girl that was hard to get,
Yet settled for the easy ones that any could claim.

I despised his inconsistency,
But admired how he ran wild.

I fell in love with his smile,
But hated I wasn't the only one putting it on his face.

I was a contradiction too—
For my heart was constantly in disarray when it belonged
to him,
And maybe that's why we sabotaged each other in the end.

But regardless,
I always liked the way he left goose bumps on my skin
And wished there was a more permanent alternative
For such a feeling of uncontrollable pleasure.

Authentic

There are things in this world that are truly authentic and teach us the main core of our true selves if only we were to listen properly—
Like your initial reaction when you're surprised by a lover's face,
What you would sacrifice for the one, who holds your heart,
Who dances in your mind once 4A.M.'s darkness haunts you?
Who lives in your dreams when sleep finally casts its spell?
What is your first thought once the sun forces your eyes open each morning,
And whose happiness do you still get on your knees and pray for, though they have become a distant memory, the same yearly birthday wish, or perhaps the rose you should have left planted firmly, instead of picking it from its roots, only to force it to wilt?

Almost

One hand on the small of my back,
The other discovering the smoothness of my cheek.
He gently guides my face to his and leans down until our
lips are parallel;
They faintly touch each other.
It is ever so light, but I can still almost taste him on my lips.
The ball is in his court now,
As I wait within his hold
Anticipating our worlds' collision.
Just waiting,
Almost there as he gets closer…
But then he stops, taking a step back.
He knows that once he gives in, there is no turning back.
Once he gives in, everything will change.
After that one kiss, there would be no stopping us.

Almost… but almost is never really enough.

Stay Away

Please stay away from me—
I am damaged and have been destroyed.
I end things without explanation.
I'll run away to a place you'll never find me.
Please don't fall in love with me—
For my love will not be tangible to your touch.

Worth Living For

I have never felt more alive than when your hands are exploring every inch of my body, every pore on my skin.
And that feeling is something worth fighting for.
That feeling, my love, is something worth *living* for.

And So We Danced

And so we danced
Under the moon.
For the first time as he spun me
Around and around,
And then it started to rain
After centuries of being caught in a drought.

Feel Something

I lie here and carefully shift through all of our old letters and love notes from our time spent together. As I read them, fragments of our past come rushing back to me. I question why I do this to myself. Why cause this much pain and confusion? The truth is, I just want to feel something... feel anything, and I would rather feel this excruciating pain and incredible sadness over our beautiful, lost love than feel nothing at all.

My Baby

My baby,
He was too afraid to tell me that he loved me,
But he didn't have to say it,
Because his eyes gave away
All of the secrets
That his soul was tired of keeping.

Summer's Sun

Summer romances always die with the summer's sun,
Once the sinful cold creeps its way in
And the winter solstice arrives just around the corner—
The days become shorter,
Nights become darker,
And love begins to dissipate.
Summer loves become mere memories.
Back when time stood still under the summer's sun,
Rich with endless possibilities
And juvenile fantasies,
Branded into us
Like a recurring dream—
Monotonous and unforgiving.

We All

We all have
Our bad days,
Our demons,
And skeletons hiding in our closets.
Everyone is susceptible.

He Didn't Say Good-bye

I don't even know how it happens, to be honest. One minute, you can't get enough of each other; you're texting back and forth each chance you get. Your life is just dragging on when you don't hear from him. You miss him. Waking up to a message from him already sets the tone for your day; a smile stretches across your face simply because you were his very first thought when he opened his beautiful eyes. Just reading the words he writes makes you want to be wrapped in his arms. The simplest of compliments from him can make you feel more valuable than you've ever felt in your entire life. There is no explaining it; you're safe. You're home. This is where you were destined to be.

But this feeling of warmth and solitude doesn't last. You'll get your "good morning" text, until one day, you don't anymore. The compliments that once made you feel so special start coming less and less frequently, until one day they just stop entirely. The home you've so proudly built for yourself within his hold suddenly crumbles, until the day comes that it is no longer yours. The spot on his chest where you would place your head late at night and the sound of his heartbeat made you feel so complete. But that too, along with everything else, is also stripped from you. Without word or reason. Gone.

You think, how can someone be so cruel—take me to places I've never been before, just to rip it all out from under me.

It happens so quickly; you ask yourself, has he really even left? He hasn't even said goodbye—
He just vanished.

You start to question your own self-value and worth. Why wasn't I enough? Did he get bored? Did he find better? Is it possible he didn't feel the same electricity that I felt when his fingers would so gently grace my skin? You come to the realization you may have lost him, and suddenly your world begins to crash, and your heart starts to split. You have questions and you need answers.

But that's just the law of this life, my dear. You may never get the closure you so desperately seek. The answers to his heartless little games may never be met. It's tragic and unfair, so your heart becomes hard for a little while. But you reach the point through your pain that you've had enough. Enough hurt, enough anguish, enough loss. So you pick yourself up off the floor, and begin to sew the broken pieces of your heart back together all on your own, until slowly but surely, you are able to begin again. You may be more cautious this time around, but you will be okay.

He Couldn't Have

Maybe, he didn't love me.

Maybe, he couldn't have loved me, because he was far too selfish and never knew the truth of what loving someone actually meant, and because of this, he didn't know what it was like to be happy, to be genuinely, immensely happy.

It was as though he faked his way through life, and that is why I had to let him go, because the truth of that reality was just so unbearably sad to me, and for my own sanity I couldn't bear to watch him self destruct any further.

I Was Wrong

I thought
That running away from him
Would force me to forget him—

But even when he was out of sight, he never was out of mind.

I Should Have Known

I guess you can say I did it to myself.
I suppose I did allow myself to fall into your trap.

I should have known.

You were just so convincing to the girl who always knew better.
Never before did I trust the tricks of the trade.
I was always one step ahead—
Until I met you, that is.
I met you, and I met my match.
Unfortunately, it wasn't the match I had always hoped for.
It was as though I was being punished for all the fools I took
before you.

I should have known.

I should have known that I would seek the karma I put out
into the universe,
But there was no preparing me for the pain.
I hate you for this hold you have on me, and I hate myself for
allowing you, and all of your insignificance to take up every
last ounce of my thoughts and emotions. What a tangled web I
have woven, all the while I get trapped even further until I am
completely stuck and about to get eaten alive in your vicious cycle.
I would have been more careful.

I should have known.

He Did Me A Favor

And once the pain subsided,
And my eyes started to dry—
I came to the realization that he did give me his best.
Sadly, his best simply wasn't enough
Because I deserved more than he was able to give,
And thus, he did me a favor,
When he left without saying goodbye.

When You Kiss My Lips

"They can never love you the way I do." He so easily expressed, his eyelids heavy from one too many beers.

I instantly wondered if he would regret this in the morning.

"They don't know you the way I do." His gaze was locked on mine.

"I don't care about any of it. It's all irrelevant—
How many hearts you've stolen, how many others have touched your skin—I have fallen in love with you for the purity of your heart, the kindness in your smile. When I look into your eyes, I swear I can touch your soul. How easily I get lost in them will always be a mystery to me. I've fallen for the simplicity in your words, in-spite of the complexity deep within your thoughts. You're beautiful, so insanely beautiful. You know you are, but you're modest and humble. You forgive more than you should, and you give out second chances like they're going out of style. You're the strongest person I've ever met. I'm actually scared of your strength, scared that you'll wake up one day and realize you don't need anyone, me included, and you'll just walk away and never look back. Don't get me wrong, I admire your strength, but I want you to know that you don't have to always be so strong on your own—I want to be the one to carry you, the one to hold you up when the weight of the world becomes too much for you to carry.

You're more stubborn than rain in a drought, and the most prideful person on the planet, but when you kiss my lips, you kiss my scars. All the pieces that were broken long before you are suddenly placed so meticulously back together again. Your lips touch mine, and I'm whole again. It's as though I was never even broken to begin with."

And just like that, I was his.

Too Good To Him

I was sick with malice of hearing it,
That I was too good to him.
It became so venomous to my ears,
That I would have preferred to be deaf.
I wanted them to see him the way I did.

They didn't know how he saved me from the cruelty of this
world.
They couldn't feel his soul,
They never knew his heart,
Because he only cared behind closed doors.
But I—
I deserved someone who would love me in the daylight,
Who would dance with me under the summer's sun,
Who would boast about the sweet wine we made together.
But he—
He only cares once the darkest hours arrive,
We only lay under the moon,
As we sip our wine in secret,
Only to taste how bitter it actually is.

Broken Heart

He ripped my heart out straight from my chest with his sharp claws.
I watched as the blood poured from my body and saturated the carpet.
Helpless, I fell to my knees and allowed the pain from a broken heart to completely soak me in.

Wild Animal

I tried holding onto something
That was never mine to keep.
You were a wild animal that was never meant to be caged,
Made to run wild with all of the other lost souls.
You were far too broken,
But I need you know that I never wanted to fix you—
I only wanted to heal you.

I'm sorry that I couldn't mend your mangled heart.

If I Had Known

If I had known that would be the last time your arms would be wrapped around me, I would have held on a little longer, grabbed you a little closer. I would have closed my eyes while I buried my head in your chest, just to hear the steadiness of your heart beat and breathe you in one last time.

If I had known that would be the last time I'd see your face, I would have starred into your eyes for a moment more. I would have memorized all the features on your face— the strength in your jaw line, the fullness of your lips, and the shyness in your crooked smile.

If I had known that would be the last time your lips would meet mine, I would have kissed you so passionately, so deeply, you'd forget to breathe in oxygen and allow it to flow to your lungs. I would pay more attention to how your hands would wander, and the way your fingers would lace within my hair. I would take it all in, the way your hand would gently grace my cheek, the way your lips lingered to my neck.

If I had known that would be the very last time you would be standing in front of me, I would have studied the smoothness in your voice, I would have carved into my brain the way you said my name and carry that around with me for the rest of my days. I would have said all the things I had been too afraid to say—

I would have forgotten all about my stubborn pride and lay it all out on the table. I swear I would have—
If only I had known.

Isn't it funny how we never know when the last time will strike? It's as though something is ours, and then it isn't. It's as though someone is here, and then they aren't. I wonder how differently we would all act if we actually took into consideration that nothing and no one is every promised, never guaranteed. They will belong only to you, until the day comes that they're gone, and then you'll contemplate what changes you would have made, if only you had known.

Envy

I envy everything that captivates your attention.
I am jealous of the sun that's privileged enough to awaken
your glowing skin,
And the stars that guide your way in the dark of night.
I am even jealous of the oxygen that fills your lungs.
I envy everything you want, need, and breathe that isn't me.

We Live In A World

We live in a world where we want what we can't have.
We want what doesn't want us.
We stand on the sidelines and watch them score with someone else,
Because we're a combination of being too proud to share how we feel,
And too fearful of being vulnerable.
We'll wait for our opportune moment to come and steal their attention,
Just praying it will in fact arrive,
And it's hypocrisy, really,
How we would rather be second best, than not an option at all.

I Am Yours

At last, I'm okay,
I have finally allowed myself to move on,
But just when I begin to believe I can live the rest of my days without your touch, you find me in my ever so careless hiding place.
With one grace of your fingers over my skin, one gentle feel of your palm over my curves, I collapse, falling back into you all over again just as I did the very first time.
I am yours.
I have been all this while.

Simple Stare

He didn't have to say it.
He didn't have to say anything at all.
I already saw it in his eyes,
In the way they so eagerly undressed me.
There was a hunger deep within them, a fire to say the least.
And with that simple stare alone, I became the student succumbing to my master.

The Fragrance

Of your sent has me hypnotized so much so, that it is hard to breathe anywhere that is absent from your presence.

Come Back

With each passing day that I don't hear from you the harder it gets to carry on, because with each passing day is a new realization that you are not coming back to me.
I will continue to wait patiently, but I am only waiting on false hopes and empty promises.

Missing Me

He told me he missed me.
Remember this feeling, I wanted to say.
Remember this feeling once my absence subsides and you become numb to my presence like you have so many times before.
Remember this feeling, when missing me becomes a thing of the past, when seeing me becomes just another part of your day.
Remember, once you become immune to my smile, how at one time all you wanted was to catch a glimpse of it—
And when you no longer crave my skin, just remember those wicked withdrawals you endured when all you needed was my touch.
They say absence makes the heart grow fonder, which is why I hide away from you for just a little while.
So when you begin to miss me, my love, just remember I will always return to you; because my biggest fear is that one day you will stop missing me and learn to live in this world without me entirely.

Dreams Of You

My heart's pounding deep within my chest, so hard that I swear it's about to burst through the rib cage that's built to protect it. Short breaths awake me as I think of you. I can't sleep because memories of you consume my brain like a predator consumes its prey. At last, I close my eyes and finally drift off amongst the clouds, but there's no escaping you, not even in my deepest slumber, because there you are even in the depths of my dreams.

Another Life

Maybe in another life, in another world, we would have made it. All of the elapsed time would be insignificant now. We would simply forget the past and let the pieces seamlessly fall back into place.

You would cook me breakfast Sunday mornings, and have my coffee already waiting before I wake. As I walk into the kitchen with sun kissed rays beaming through the window, waking my sleepy eyes, there you will be standing. Spatula in one hand, you'd gaze over your shoulder to throw me that half smile I fell in love with. I'll walk over to you and wrap my arms around your bare body. Hugging you from behind, I'll gently kiss your skin, and then place my cheek against your back, taking in all of your warmth.

We would go for long drives in your car, windows rolled down, and music blasting, the wind blowing through my hair. We would get lost in our passionate conversations, while you'd steal intimate glances of me instead of focusing on the road. I'd sing out loud to Genesis and The Temptations, and pretty soon after a few minutes of pretending to be too cool, you'd give in and be singing right along with me. Right beside me, one hand on the wheel, the other tangled in mine.

Things with you were just always so easy, always so right... why did it take me so long to see? I never would have let you go, and you never would have found her. You'd tell me you

38

love me, and I'd say it back this time. I would have realized the magnitude of what I had, and cherished you and all you gave me, just as you always hoped I would. I would keep you forever. You would be mine and I would be only yours—

Maybe, in another life.

Justifications

And when you reappeared on the darkest night
You reminded me of our unfinished business—
You came back flaunting justifications,
Full of regrets—
Soiled on your skin from when you walked away.

Believer

"I lived my life as a nonbeliever, up until the day I met her, that is,
Because something of that caliber of perfection could only be created by a higher power—
She brought me to God."

See Me

What else can I do to make you see me?
These days, no matter how many times you look, you're staring straight through me.
Once upon a time that's not how our story went,
Our eyes would meet and instantaneously we would be captivated by each other.
Your hunger for me was more than apparent, and I foolishly craved you right in return.
I feel like I am nailed to the ground with this hold you have over me.
There is nothing I wouldn't do to regain what has been lost between us,
Just to have you look at me the way you once did,
The way you used to see right into me,
And physically touch my soul.
I guess I always was a little too much like glass—
Whether you were looking into my soul, or through it,
You were always capable of seeing past me.
I'm just as fragile
And even break just as easily…
But I need you to know that this is not over for me.

Everything I am and everything I do, is all for you.

False Fantasies

With him
I imagined a life that I thought was tangible,
A life that I could hold in my hand
And lace my delicate fingers around—
Beautiful visions that I later learned
Can only exist in dreams.

Letting You Go

I just had to let you go.

I swear I didn't want to, but it's what I had to do.

The more I knew you, the harder I fell, and the more I started to love you—but the more I loved you, the more I began to *need* you. I began to depend solely on you to make me happy, to make me want to exist. You were my fix; I was constantly high when I was with you, indestructible to the world. Nothing could take me down, well except for you, of course, and thus the beginning of the end began to form. The more your power grew over me, the deeper I fell under your spell, and the farther away I started to fall from myself. I forgot who I was, and became so detached from me.

I just really need you to know that this wasn't your fault; it was mine—

Mine, for making you so significant.

Mine, for making you more important than anything else I could touch.

Mine, for being satisfied only when I had your attention and approval.

Mine, for just so easily handing you my heart, allowing you to do with it what you pleased.

Mine, for being so naïve to think it wouldn't break in your hands.

It was too much pressure, holding you responsible, and I see now that wasn't fair, it was too much to ask for.

I had to slip away; I had to let you go. I just simply had to survive. Please forgive me.

Despite Your Flaws

It wasn't just in the way you said my name and allowed each letter to roll off your tongue.
It wasn't only with your hand in mine, loving me fully with each waking breath,
Or when your smile alone changed my entire life around.
It was even when the desires of your heart steered you away from me—
When each piece of your soul began to love each piece of me a little less,
And even when the selfishness of the will to your way overpowered what you once bloomed for me.
Even then, you were all I longed for, all I loved. All I knew.
As you drifted further into the distance, I had no choice, but only to love you more desperately, just fighting to hold on.

Checkmate

He said all the right things and played all the right moves, so strategically until he had me right where he wanted.

When my hair would fall in front of my face, he would gracefully tuck the strand behind my ear, just to get a better look into my eyes, and easier access to my lips.

When he would look through the windows to my soul, I'd swear he could see every letter I had ever written, every dream I ever uttered.

When I would cry, he kissed my tears.

He fed onto each word I spoke as though they were nourishment for his own body.

He was a true gentleman, nothing less and nothing more.

Little did I know I was just another piece to the game he was playing.

He was the king, protected by all his knights and bishops as he hid behind his words and false gestures of hopes.

I never even stood a chance.

He turns to me with the slyest grin.
"Checkmate."

He had won yet again.

Relapse

Why can't either one of us stay away?
We do so well for so long, until we just can't seem to take it any longer.
Sooner or later, we fall back into each other's arms instantaneously.
Too much time escapes me, and I begin to miss what we used to have.
Desperate, I can't help but to relapse, only to feel the beauty of this high and the destruction of this addiction all at once.

I Can Still

I can still taste his lips on mine.
I can still feel his heat against my body.
I still smell his cologne on my pillow.
I still feel his breath on my neck, his hands in my hair, and his fingers gently grazing down my spine.
His hands on my skin are still so present.
It's been a long time since I have actually felt his touch, yet I close my eyes and still feel him, all of him, at every waking moment.

Devil In Disguise

He was the devil in disguise.
It was in the way he smoothly spoke,
The way he was able to make me do anything he wanted.
All he had to do was say the word and it was already done.
The way he made me question everything I had ever known.
I changed for him.
I just wanted to be enough for him.
But I wasn't. I was never going to be, and no other woman
was bound to be either,
Because his heart will always be meant to stray—it simply
wasn't built to belong to one woman alone.
He came dressed as an angel and claimed to be sent from
God himself.
I could have sworn he was going to save me from my sins,
But he was only the devil in disguise,
Whose only mission was to corrupt a young girls' innocence,
And drag me to hell with him.

Best-kept Secret

You were my best-kept secret.

I believe the thrill of no one knowing is the very thing that kept us alive for so long.

Meeting at our hideaway that the world would never know, Pulling me up against you, staining my neck with your lips, Sneaking away from the chaos, only to be alone with every inch of you.

Even I didn't know the magnitude of my affections for you until it was too late, until we were too far in, but by this time, I was too proud to say how I felt.

Now do you see, my dear? I too had a secret I was keeping from you.

I almost wish those four walls could talk, only to have another witness of all the magic we made.

So, you will forever be my best-kept secret, in every beautifully tragic way possible.

Poison

When you know something is poison, toxic to your body, you're supposed to stay away from it, right? Yet at the same time, there's something so hypnotizing about having something you're not supposed to. Just one little bite of the forbidden fruit, just one tiny taste—that's all you want at first, just to see what you're missing. But sooner or later, that taste won't be enough. You will begin to crave it endlessly, until you end up eating the entire fruit, allowing the poison to spread through your veins, and absolutely kill you.

I'm Sorry

I'm sorry if I ever made you feel underappreciated, unwanted.
I'm sorry if you ever felt second best.
But you should know, I need you to know that you made me feel alive when I felt like I was dying.
You loved me when I didn't even like myself.
You saw the best in me when I couldn't even find the tiniest speck of goodness.
You lifted me up when I was falling.
You saved my life.
And for all of these things, I am grateful.
But my gratitude will never be enough,
Because I will never love you the way you need me to,
And I so selfishly want to continue to hold on,
But you will always want more than I can offer.
And because of this, I need to say goodbye.

I Had You Once

I had you once,
I let you go.
You moved on,
I did not know,
That I would lose someone so great—
I guess it wasn't in my fate.
Seeing you now is so hard to do.
My heart always stops, right on cue.
Knowing you've moved on makes me sick.
Was she really your last pick?
They say you don't know what you have till its gone.
This saying is the truth, not just a con.
I had you once,
I let you go.
You moved on,
I did not know,
That you held the special token—
And without it,
I would always be so broken.

Alone

I sit here alone with nothing left to do but allow the tears to stream down my cheeks, and watch as they stain the pages of the letters I attempt, but fail to write you.

The pen touches the page, but the ink won't seem to flow.

Numb, broken, and falling apart piece by piece, you have taken everything, including my soul with you and I have nothing—nothing left to give to you.

Run

I was supposed to run.
I know I was.
That's what we are supposed to do when we encounter
things we know will cause us pain.
So why is it that I gravitated towards him instead?
It was unexplainable, how the moment I first laid eyes on
him, it was as though we were already connected,
Like he was already a part of me from another world, in
another life.
It was like I already knew the outcome and the brokenness
he would cause me.
I guess he was inevitably in my fate,
My tragic destiny—

I suppose I wasn't meant to run.

Nicky Arnstein

It was a year in the making,
After all the flirtation and all that fixation.
On a cool May night, it finally happened
He leaned me against the car, pulling me in close with his hand intertwined in my hair.
When his lips met mine, they fit so perfectly, so beautifully without even trying, without even forcing it.
I can still feel his wine stained lips lingering to my cheeks, my nose, and neck.
My very own Nicky Arnstein,
So smooth, so debonair.
And just in the same Nicky style, he kissed me so magically and then disappeared, the perfect vanishing act.
But before he goes, the perfect gentleman opens the car door and sees me in.
I know this is not a goodbye, just a see you later, leaving me with the most beautiful remembrance of him.
But when we meet again, because we always will, I'll tell him how I wish he had called.
How I wish he hadn't waited so long in the first place, and how I wish he didn't let so much time go by now.
Maybe one day we'll meet in the middle and finally end up together, just like Nicky and Fanny—the perfect gentleman with the not so perfect funny girl.
Maybe we'll suffer the same tragic fate they once shared,
Or maybe we'll beat the odds, if only *My Nicky* sticks around long enough to find out.

4:01 a.m.

It's 4:01 in the morning and I'm feeling the wine spill through my pores—
It is not the wine that has me drunk; it is being haunted by your undying presence.

Can't Stay Away

I just can't seem to stay away.
Your presence alone is addicting,
Your scent alone is nourishing,
Your kiss alone—oh that kiss—it's simply hypnotizing.
Your lips on mine are all I seem to think about these days.
Onlookers, I'm sure, think I'm foolish.
But it's okay,
Because I just cant seem to stay away.
Being around you has become my new normal—
So perfect,
So catastrophic.
Knowing that I will see you gets me through the harshness
of my week,
And the destruction of my days.
Seeing your face and bright brown eyes makes it better,
Makes it all worth it.
It's okay,
As long as I'm in your arms by the end of my treacherous
days.

It Wasn't Fair

It wasn't fair to call me your sunshine,
To tell me how my smile would brighten your day.

It wasn't fair to notice every detail on my face,
Every beauty mark on my skin—
To think even my flaws were still so miraculous.

It wasn't fair to have the most captivating soul
To match your perfect features;
To be the farthest thing from shallow,
And the closest thing to humble.

It wasn't fair to kiss me with such passion.
To run your gentle touch through my pores
And explore every inch of my soul.

It wasn't fair to pursue me in the way that you did,
Knowing damn well that we could never be.

It wasn't fair that once our souls genuinely began to
intertwine, you pulled away, desperately attempting to cut
ties in hopes of protecting us both in the long run.

It wasn't fair that once I was finally able to live with the
distance *you* put in place, is when you realized you could no
longer resist all the temptation between us.

It wasn't fair that you returned to me just as I was officially
letting go.
How selfish of you to reappear just as I was beginning to
learn how to live without you.

Let's Pretend

Let's pretend we're both still happy.
Let's pretend when we lay our heads down to rest, it is each other we still dream about.
Let's pretend when I unlock the door, you'll be right behind it awaiting my arrival.
Let's pretend our hearts hadn't turned to stone.
Let's pretend this isn't goodbye, but a casual see you later instead.

Trouble

You did warn me, after all.
Once it was too late and we were both already too far in.
You confessed how deeply you craved me, but you would purposely keep a safe distance between us, just enough, you would say.

You were trouble. You told me so yourself. You warned me to stay away.
But I couldn't.
I wanted to, believe me I did
But the gravitation I felt, like a magnetic force pulling us together was simply too much to bear.
I wasn't strong enough to withstand you.
I craved the taste of your lips more than you could ever know.
I was never safer than when I was wrapped securely in your arms.
I was at my happiest when you were kissing me with everything you had, when you would burry your flawless face into my neck and gracefully kiss my skin.

I wanted you.
I wanted all of you, all of the beautiful parts and all of the less than perfect parts.
I wanted to nurture your demons
And kiss your flaws.

Maybe I couldn't fix them all, but I thought, if only I could patch them up for a little while, maybe I could heal you for just a little while... maybe then, it could be enough.

But you knew yourself far better than I did,
And you already knew what dead-end desires my heart was fantasizing about.
No matter how much you cared,
No matter how strong your feelings for me were, despite everything, it simply would just never be enough.
You are who you are and your womanizing ways will always be a part of you; your dirty little tricks and games will always outweigh the honesty and integrity that's meant to build a relationship.
You will never be capable of belonging to one woman alone.
You were trouble. You told me so yourself.
If only I had listened, if only I had walked away when you begged me to, if only I had stopped my heart from developing something that would never be reciprocated, maybe then, it wouldn't be so broken and unfixable now.

When I Died

Right before my eyes he took her hand instead of mine.
Right before his eyes, everything inside of me started to die.

She's Not Me

Please tell me, how does it feel to know that you will forever be haunted by my presence, even through my absence?
That regardless of how beautiful she is, or how bright her smile shines, she will never hold a candle to what we had.
She will still never be me.
It won't be her you want sitting in your passenger seat, sharing your soul with—
It will be me.
Your lips will never fit as beautifully together as ours did.
Her touch will never stimulate your senses quite like mine did.
No matter how hard she tries, she won't be me.
No matter how much you pretend, you will never be *us*.
You see, I will be okay, one day.
I, will bring myself to move on,
Because I was always more than what you deserved.
But you—
You must live with the repercussions of the damage you've left behind.
You will be forced to carry me around with you.
I have left my stain on you,
A stain that will forever remain.
I will always haunt you—
The ghost of me will never leave you.

His Lips

He kissed my collarbone
Like sweet nectar had been flowing from it
And with his lips,
Left a trail of passion tracing over every unknown inch of
my skin until he stripped away my fear, and left me no choice
but to succumb to all of my apprehensions.
He touched my heart and captured my soul, and with that
he had me right where he wanted me to be all along.

Fear

I thought you were my saving grace,
But I was so wrong.
Instead of making things better, you only made them
worse—
Adding much more stress and fear than I had ever endured.
Constantly living in fear—
Fear that I would lose you,
Fear that I would never be enough,
Fear that I would be in constant competition with every
other woman around me,
And you did this to me.
It thrilled you to be the puppet master, pulling on the strings
to my heart,
Laughing, as you watched me desperately do anything to
keep you,
Secretly knowing that all of my fears were validated.
All of my fears eventually came to light.

This Man Of Mine

This man of mine who makes me feel so alive,
Who makes even my darkest day shine brighter,
Who is able to manage a smile upon my face even through
the tears I cry—
This man of mine is going to take me down.
I can feel myself drowning, but I can't seem to stay afloat.
This man of mine is pulling me deeper and deeper, straight
down to the very bottom.
I can no longer see the surface.
I can only see darkness now—I am in too deep.
This man of mine will be the death of me.

Naïve

I hate how naïve I allowed myself to be when it came to you.
After our very first encounter, I promised myself I wouldn't
fall for you,
No matter how special you made me feel,
Or the words you would feed my ego,
I promised myself I wouldn't cave.
I assured my mother she raised me smarter than that,
Than to fall for such an obvious player who would only know
how to crush me,
And never love me.
But the more I got to know you; I just needed to have you,
The deeper I could feel myself falling.
So I finally took my final leap off the cliff,
And gracefully placed my heart within your hold,
Then I watched as you crumbled it within your fist.
How foolish I had been—
So naïve I allowed myself to be when it came to you.

Self-Control

They were amazed by my self-control and my will to withstand your temptation.

They were amazed by my ability to turn off my feelings for you just as easily as they came to me in the first place.

They were amazed that your tricks and games didn't work on me, for I was smarter than that—

If only they knew that I was only pretending, their amazement would more than likely subside.

The truth is, that it took every single last thing in my soul not to give in to my passions and desires when it came to you.

The truth is, that my feelings for you were far stronger than they had ever been for another; it was as though I was living for you. Hell, I would have even died for you.

The truth is, that I did indeed fall for every last word your lips ever uttered.

I got so deep, so far in, that you were actually swallowing me whole and you didn't even know it. You didn't even know the power you had over me—

Simply because I am such a good pretender, don't you see?

Why We Do What We Do

I will never fully understand why we do what we do.
We create such an amount of distance between the two of
us—
Months without speaking or exchanging even an ounce of
interaction at all,
Only to discover how immensely we miss one another.
I am not sure if it's simply to see if we are able to live without
each other,
Or if our stubborn pride just gets in the way, so we spite
ourselves—
Because neither one of us wants to accept
That we do in fact need each other,
In order to function in this heartless world.

Chameleon

He was a chameleon who was anything I needed him to be.
When I was stranded, he always came to get me.
When my heart was cold, he knew how to make it warm again.
When I was lost, he always knew where I would be found.
He would kiss where I hurt, and make my world better again.
But most importantly, he was my hero and he was always saving me, you see.
No matter what situation I managed to become tangled in,
He always rescued me.

The Same Man

When she told me she had developed feelings for you, my entire body went numb.

My hands started shaking in the same rapid rhythm my heart was racing.

What do I say to my friend who has feelings for the same man I love?

The same man I would speak to from the moment the sun would rise, to the very instant the stars took their place—

The first man to ever see me naked in every humanly way possible,

The only man whose fingertips know every flaw and imperfection on my skin.

The man who makes my entire body quiver with the satisfying taste of his lips—

I say nothing,

Because the secret of you, and I, and the beauty of what we once shared will be buried with me, with you, with us.

I say nothing, but die inside each time your name leaves her lips, sitting in silence as I am forced to picture the two of you tangled together.

When You're Not Here

Hate takes over my heart when I think of your bad behavior
when I'm not near,
Like in this very moment, all I can think about is what you're
up to—
Where are you?
Who's touching your skin, exploring all the parts of you that
belong to me?
Whose bed are you taking over?
Who is lying next to you in my place?
Over thinking, over analyzing every word, every detail,
My mind just can't seem to escape the worst.
But then I will see you again.
You will kiss the corner of my mouth,
Then softly kiss my lips,
While lacing your fingers with mine.
My bitter feelings will fade away,
For I will only be happy with you by my side.

Simplicity

I didn't ask for much really—
I just wanted him to lead me while we danced in the rain,
And kiss me with such passion, that it would feel as though
he were stealing oxygen from my lungs for his own survival.

You Didn't Notice

I pulled away just a little bit,
Just enough to see if you would notice—
If you would even come after me.
I did leave the door open for you, after all.
But you never came knocking.
Hell, I don't even think you noticed that I never closed it all the way,
And that it's still ever so slightly open, until this very day.

The Moment

The moment our eyes met I actually felt my heart skip a beat—
For I had never witnessed a face more beautiful, had never felt such an immense amount of instant chemistry for another soul.
I truly believed that with a face like that it was inevitable for your heart to always wander, never to settle down.
You were smooth,
You were charming,
You were trouble,
You were every woman's desire.
I was smart enough to keep you at arm's length, created by the fear of becoming another notch in your belt, another woman captivated under your spell.
I did so well for so long until I just couldn't hold back any longer, and submissively gave in to all my desires.
I forgot to stop my heart from latching onto you,
Disregarded the thought of how painful falling for you would be,
Didn't think to mention that I could never fully recover.

My Favorite Part

My favorite part of my everyday is only a small moment of time, when I finally have him all to my selfish little self. He softly kisses me, but before I leave him, he gazes into my eyes with that look that says, *"I'm falling in love with you and I promise I'm trying so desperately with everything inside of me not to hurt you,"* and with that endearing, complex look, I can't help but to fall even deeper.

That look—

It gets me every time.

The One That Got Away

I am sitting here allowing my tears to run down my cheeks,
Because I have finally been struck with the realization that
I have been avoiding all of these years—
That after all of this time, I did always truly believe that you
were the one,
The only one,
And that, we would realize how desperately we need each
other—
How our love would ultimately be enough.
We would inevitably be meant to live happily ever after,
After all the sadness,
And all of the games.
It just wouldn't matter, and we would be happy.
But you're still stuck in your ways,
And I see the sadness behind your eyes when you look at me,
Because you know I cannot wait forever.
I will be forced to move on eventually, leaving you behind.
I don't want to be your one that got away.
Please don't ruin this for me.
Please don't ruin this for us.

You Promised

Do you remember that night you promised you wouldn't hurt me?
I think about it all the time, my dear, how you took my hand in yours and held it so tightly as you locked my gaze.
The thing that astonishes me till this very day, is that you did, indeed, keep that promise.
You didn't hurt me—
You ran away, as fast as your feet would go before you could.
And I am haunted still,
Because you robbed me of being able to make my own decisions when it came to us—you made up my mind for me.
I guess you thought it would be easier this way, less painful to just rip the band-aid off quick and easy.
But being left with this disappointment and unknown
Is far worse than any damage you could have left behind.
It's sad to me you didn't trust yourself enough to love me,
It's sad, that now we will never really know—
We will forever be taunted by what if's and broken promises, of what *could have been.*

Lifesaver

I clung to his words like a lifesaver thrown to me while I was drowning.

"I will not hurt you."

I clung to them for dear life, praying that they would save me.

Afraid

"What are you so afraid of?" I needed to know.

"You."

I saw the fear penetrating from his eyes.

"I am afraid of not being enough for you."

His honesty left me speechless.

My gaze was locked ferociously on his.

I couldn't think of the words to speak, what do I say?

My silence spoke louder than any words ever could.

We both knew the truth hidden behind his words, though neither of us wanted to face them.

It was then, in that tempting moment that I grabbed his face and kissed his lips, kissed him like I never have before.

In that moment, I didn't care what our future held.

I didn't care what was right from wrong.

Maybe if I kissed him passionately enough, I could kiss the demons right out of him.

I wanted him,

And I needed him to know just how badly.

I Would Choose You

I would choose you,
Through a thousand lifetimes,
And a billion galaxies—
Across every ocean,
And each mountain's tallest peak.
Through it all,
I would still choose you.

3:24 A.M.

At 3:24A.M. you passionately pushed me up against the doorframe and kissed me.

As you opened my mouth with your own, all of the feelings and emotions we've been holding onto for so long flowed so seamlessly together, straight into each other's souls, completely taking over our bodies.

Two entities suddenly becoming one.

After all this time, there we were, at 3:24am in the exact position we were desperately avoiding, yet anticipating at the same time.

At 3:24A.M. you told me that all you wanted was to experience the taste of my lips and hold my body close to yours.

You wanted nothing less, and nothing more.

At 3:24A.M. I knew I should have left running, for I knew too much temptation would come from being alone with the most gorgeous man I had ever seen who just happened to have the most captivating soul I had ever encountered.

I should have left, but something stopped me.

Maybe it was the fire burning behind your deep brown eyes for me,

Or the way your skin felt so smoothly against my own.

It could have been the way I craved your breath against my neck as you left traces of soft kisses on my skin,

Or the satisfying intensity of you biting my lower lip.

Whatever it was, it had me in a trance, never wanting to leave this intimate moment.

I took everything in, memorizing every delicate detail from that night.

But now it is 3:24A.M., and I am lying in my bed alone, numb to all of the outside noise.

I can't sleep as my mind runs wild, desperately trying to fit the pieces to the broken puzzle back together again, hoping that it could tell me where we went wrong.

I should have known better than to hold on to empty promises and lost words of hope.

I should have known better than to believe a single word that came out of that beautiful mouth of yours,

I should have known better than to believe the actions of a man in lust at 3:24A.M.

Dreaming Again

As I open my heavy eyes while the sun creeps its way through the window pane, I am struck by the realization that you are not laying next to me, that I have in fact wasted yet another night dreaming of you with sad hopes that will never be reached—

For your flawless face is just a distant memory now that I could only vividly see as sleep takes over my soul.

He inspired me in more ways than he could ever know,
In more ways that even I cannot fathom.

Selfless

I watched as his want for her and need to have her consumed everything in his entire being. I watched as he desperately attempted to change the man he's been all of these years in order to please her, and to ultimately keep her.

She was everything he had ever wanted, an angel sent in the form of his perfect woman, but the deeper he fell the clearer the realization became that she was far too good for him. Despite how hard he fought, he could never become the man she needed; the man he wanted to be, and with that he did the most selfless thing a man in love could possibly do, and cut all ties with the woman who deserved more before she was able to fall just as deep as he had.

He was far too gone you see, too set in his ways from so many years of manipulation and meaningless one night stands, that he forgot, he too, deserved more. If only she had come a few years sooner when he was still pure, before the world corrupted a young man's innocence and groomed him to become the player he is now, running the game with such charisma—just a few years sooner and maybe, just maybe they would have stood a chance.

Every Detail

I know every detail on your body,
Every single beauty mark on your skin.
I have traced over each of them thousands of times in my brain,
Counting each as I connect the dots like constellations in the sky.
I know every line on your face,
And how each is a reminder of the hard life you left behind.
I could write an entire novel about the scar on your upper lip,
And how it's the most beautiful imperfection I have ever seen,
And I would be satisfied kissing that scar as long as you'd let me.

Lost

They say that time heals all wounds, but I can't grasp the day that time will heal these deep scars you have left upon my heart.

They say this too shall pass, but this pain I have engraved in my soul from the day you walked away will be left with me for all of eternity.

I cannot see a future when I will no longer crave your touch; your soft kisses on my lips.
My mornings are the hardest, for I do not want to get out of my bed and face another day without you.

That pain in my heart,
That sharpness in my stomach,
It is all too real when you are not here.

I have lost so much of myself in you—
So much of myself that will be lost in forever.

Toxic Behavior

There was just so much below the surface that was wrong
with our picture—
All of the jealousy,
Stubbornness,
Spitefulness,
Pride.
But despite it all, we were still so painfully addicted to each
other;
The way a leech latches on to human flesh was the same
toxic way he had latched onto me, and he didn't finally
squirm away, letting me be, until he was sure he had sucked
out every last piece of my soul, which he is still carrying
around with him, till this very day.

Inevitable

We were both learning to live with the distance between us, but it wasn't what either of us actually wanted. The time apart was paining him so, I just couldn't stand to watch it any longer.

I ran to him, wrapping my arms around him.

Nose to nose he grabbed my face as we kissed; all of the months of separation flowed through that kiss.

It took everything in his being, but he backed away and looked into my eyes,

With fear,

With pain,

With disappoint, within himself mostly.

Naturally, this would not end well. He will burn me, it was inevitable and we both knew it.

He couldn't help it—He was fire and I was the moth to his flame.

"I'm not good for you." he finally let out.

"I don't care," I whispered. "If I'm going to get hurt, I desperately want it to be by you."

This was only a dream...

Can We Go Back

I just so painfully want to go back to the way things were—
When I was yours, and all was still right with the world.
When the moment you'd see me, was the moment my day began.
When you would hold my face in your hands, and passionately kiss me.
When you couldn't even walk past me without placing your lips on my cheek.
When there was something so beautiful and sensual behind your eyes when they would stare into mine—The way you would look at me with an undeniable sense of security, like I was the only thing that existed in your entire world.
All of these things, all of these little yet magical things that made me fall in love with you, God, I miss them. I miss them so much.

Thoughts Of You

All my problems begin once I lay my head to rest on my pillow late at night. It takes me hours to simply fall asleep because all I think about is you,
All of the beautiful times we had,
How perfect we could have been if only we learned to behave properly,
Where exactly it is we first went wrong.

Once I finally drift off, my brain is automatically attacked by images of you. Your gorgeous face and perfectly sculpted structure is all I see, even while I am dreaming.
I dream of old fights we once had,
Each ending differently.
I imagine what else I could have said, how I could have kept you.

Then, as I am finally about to be wrapped in your arms and kissed the way I have been longing for, kissed the way I have been missing for all of this time, I open my eyes only to come to the horrific realization that it was only a dream; and so begins the vicious cycle all over again, with you being my very first thought as I open my eyes each morning, to the very last thing I see as I close them night in, and night out.

If Only

If only you could see yourself through my eyes,
You would see just how perfect you really are.
If only you could see your full potential,
You would see how capable you are of reaching every dream
you ever dreamt.
If only you could see the power within your touch,
Then you would heal every soul who stepped into your life.
If only you could see that when I see you, I see my future,
You would be mine, because you would see that otherwise,
you were only wasting time.

Stupid

I came home alone,
Because you went home with another.
Now, I'm curled up in my bed,
As my tears are hitting these pages,
Replaying everything we had—
Everything we were,
From beginning to end;
Where it started,
And where it stopped.
How one day you were all for me,
And then one day you just weren't anymore.
How could I have been so stupid?
To think anything you said had truth behind it?
My gut told me there were other women,
I just never thought I'd have to witness it firsthand for myself.
And it was killing me. God, it was killing me to see you with her.
You knew it was, too.
Watching as you picked her up using the same exact methods that once made me feel so special, leading me straight into your arms.
How, oh how, could I have been so stupid?

Incoherent

I am a prisoner of my own mind.
I have become obsessed and incoherent,
Unable to make any type of logic, or sense of us.

My *Nicky Arnstein*

I felt like a teenager once again,
As you chased me down the street for a simple hello;
But two hours later, we have lost track of time.
It is time for me to go, and you had to get back to the monotony of your job.
How I mustn't ever forget my mother turning to me and saying, "Oh boy. You can get in a lot of trouble with that one."
"My God, *I already am* in trouble."
It was as though I were a schoolgirl again, as butterflies fluttered their wings in my stomach.
Momma always knows best.
Why didn't I listen to her?

Moved On

You have moved on,
I see it in everything that you no longer do.
Your eyes no longer light up when they meet with mine.
You don't look at me with the same heat and passion you once did.
You no longer shed compliments,
And your jealous outbursts have disappeared,
As well as your territorial ways.
You have stopped caring about what I do,
Because you have moved on.
I pray that this isn't an occasion of lost love,
Just something that you had to do.
Hopefully one day, I will move on too.

Please

Please don't tell me that I meant nothing.
Please tell me that what we had was so beautiful, so special,
that it kills you every single day you walk this earth that you
had to loose it.
Please tell me you think about me all the time, as much as
I do you.
Please tell me no other girl will ever compare to me.
Please tell me you loved me,
Because I love you, I did then. I do now.
I will never stop loving you.

Do Anything

I would do absolutely anything to feel his lips on mine once more.
Call me crazy,
But I would endure any amount of his sadistic torture to be kissed like that again,
Even if it was for only one last time.
I would take it,
I would embrace it,
Simply because I haven't stopped craving it.

Our Last

He kissed me.
Again.
Just as he had so many times before.
But it's been a little while, you see, for he has tried to stay away, from me, from us, from what we could one day be—
The good, bad, or ugly.
And I respect that, his intentions are good, the purest they could possibly be, when it comes to me.
So he tries so desperately to stay away,
Only for my own good.
But he can't.
He just keeps failing.
This kiss was beautiful.
It was also tragic.
He wraps his arms around me to say goodnight, and kisses only the corner of my mouth.
As he begins to pull away, he looks into my eyes and leans in for a simple peck,
But now that he's tasted me, it just isn't enough.
Suddenly, we are both lost deep within this perfect kiss—
His hands in my hair,
I'm too focused on his lips that I forget where mine are.
I can feel everything flowing from his pores, straight into my soul.
His pain,
His fears,
His lust,

His love,
His guilt.
He can't resist me, or I him.
I have longed for his lips for what feels like an eternity,
I have missed his kisses more than he will ever know.
I take in this moment and cherish it so, because this—
This will be our last kiss.

Limbo

We are in limbo.
I don't know what he wants.
Hell, I don't even know what I want.
All I know for sure is that I have never wanted to be so accepted by anyone in my entire life.
I just want him to want me.

Means Something

Any other man wouldn't have been so tortured about a
simple kiss,
But he was.
It was something he wanted so desperately,
But it was killing him at the same time.
It meant something to him—
And because it meant anything to him, it was absolutely
everything to me.

Beauty Comes From Pain

I have come to realize that some of my most beautiful, purest self-reflecting moments have surfaced through my absolute darkness.

In conclusion: beauty, in the highest form, stems from pain. And I have you to thank for that.

Holding Him Back

I was holding you back—
And I didn't even realize that I was doing so,
Until I walked a few steps ahead just to see if you would
follow.
But you didn't.
You noticed long before I that we could never work out the
way we wanted to.
We were incompatible, and you were only trying to cut the
weight before we both sank even deeper.
You were trying to let me go,
But I was never one to leave without putting up a fight.
I was playing God, trying to control a situation that just
wasn't meant to be.
I was playing with our fate, and that wasn't fair to either of
us.
It wasn't until I fully took myself out of the situation that I
was able to see clearly through your eyes.
You were being selfless.
And I—
Well I was being selfish.

Numb

I am just sitting here alone,
Staring out my window,
Onto the lake
And watching as the water so gracefully reflects off my bedroom ceiling,
As the moon's perfect reflection causes inconsistent waves throughout.
I cannot help but to compare this perfect sight to our imperfect love affair—
Filled with beauty, pain and inconsistency.
In this moment, I can't help but to feel so disconnected
From you,
From myself,
From everything in my existence.
I am not sad, necessarily,
Just numb.

Will She Know?

I constantly wonder, as I sit curled up in the comfort of my bed, writing about you, crying out to you, if she will ever read the words I write, and without having any clear certainty in her soul, will she still know? Will my words leave her with a familiar, yet empty reminder? Will she still know that this man I continue to speak of through my writings is the very same man who belongs to her now? That her man has hurt me so, causing me to spill all of the brokenness he has left behind onto these bare pages, consuming them in the same toxic way he once consumed me...

What did he see in her soul that didn't live in mine?

Empty

I dreamt of you last night,
But I woke up empty this morning
Tangled in my cotton sheets,
Lost in this queen size bed.
Alone.
I just wanted you here with me.
I just wanted your face to be the first thing I saw when I
opened my eyes,
But instead I was struck by the absolute emptiness of these
cold white walls.

Home

And when you pass my house on your late night drive,
Just know that there I will be waiting for you.
I know you cannot resist glancing towards my bedroom window to see if the light is still on,
But just know that it will be.
The eternal flame will always stay burning bright as your sign that it has all been forgiven, that it will be okay to come knocking again, even if it is just for one last time.
I promise, I would always let you back in.
You can always come home again.

I Know You

I know you,
I know your soul.
I know all your pieces that nobody else is allowed to see—
The pieces that you have tried so hard to hide away from
the rest of the world,
But despite your efforts, I still see them.
I know every single last one of them.
I have carefully dissected each piece so perfectly.
No other will ever be able to see you the way I do.
No other will ever want you in your rawest form quite the
way that I do,
And because you hold me on your pedestal, no other will
ever compare to the way I'm seen through your damaged
eyes.

Numb To Me

He is numb to me now.
There is no more excitement behind his eyes.
He is always expecting me behind every turn,
Around every corner.
I wish I could escape and hide away for just a little while—
But because he knows my heart, and he knows my soul,
He will always know exactly where to find me.

Last Kiss

You are the last kiss to have graced my lips,
And I can't help but to think of all the kisses you have had since mine.
I can't bear to have another touch my skin.

I wonder, if I am ever able to bring myself to move on, if my next man will be able to taste you on my lips.
Will he become acquainted with all the fragments of you left behind—
The traces of scars you have left on my body?
Will he be able to heal them, love them in all of their destruction?
Or will he only add to the pain?

Thorns

I needed something to hold on to,
So I took in his promises that looked like roses,
Only to get pricked by their thorns.

Everything

I am everything you ever wanted, but never had because you couldn't handle.
You needed something that you could hold captive in your hand,
Something you could control,
Something you could tame.
But I was never the submissive type, you see,
And even when I wanted to be something you would be proud to call your own, my stubbornness got in the way, refusing to allow me to become something outside of myself.
If you were unable to handle my soul and all that it was in actuality, then you weren't capable of having me in any form.
We were just incompatible—
And you could never change me, the same way I could never change you.
I admit, that I wanted desperately to change you; only to make our broken pieces fit beautifully together in order to complete the perfect puzzle,
But I now know that you can't fix someone who doesn't believe they are broken.

I Can't Be

I can't be cold to the one man, who single handedly warms
my soul,
Who moves mountains in my heart with only one look.
No matter what he does to me, I see him, and my heart can't
help but to smile.
I endured so much pain when it came to him,
All of which I would repeat on command if it meant being
near him a minute more.
I should hate him, but I could never bring myself to.

It is an unexplainable curse, to love something so fully that
can only love you halfway in return.

With You

He asked me where my head was.

It was not with him, although he was the one laying beside me.

It was with you, thinking back on the night I left my hat at our spot, and returned the very next day—the way your eyes lit up when they met with mine once you spotted me from across the room. As I left that night, you took my hand and walked me outside. I remember the comfort from the warmth of your lips on my rosy cheek on that cold February night.

My head was with you, as I replayed our very first kiss. I always wished I could go back to relive that moment. It was something we had both waited for, for so long after a year of playing cat and mouse. It was the start of something so beautiful and pure before we turned it into tragedy.

My head was with you, as I thought about the night you told me you had fallen for me. You took a quick break from kissing me to speak those words and before I could respond, you continued. You always kissed me in order to stop me from speaking, and it worked every time. I so easily got lost in you, and your lips.

My head was with you, caught in the moment when we danced in the rain. It was pouring as you sat there watching me twirl around by myself. I grabbed your hand to pull you up, and without resistance, we began to beautifully intertwine as the rain continued to stain us.

My head was with you, reliving our very last kiss. I could read your body language, for it had been a little while since your lips last met mine, and I could clearly see how much you wanted to taste them again, how lonely your lips had been without mine, and as they did meet again, in that moment, there was magic.

It was a living contradiction, for in that moment it felt as though an eternity passed, as well as no time at all; It felt as though everything was perfectly back in place, yet falling apart all over again; having everything that had been taken from me come pouring back, only to know I would lose it all as quickly as it returned.

I constantly pray that our story is still unwritten; that God will bring us together again.

So, when he asks me where my head is, just know that it is with you. It will always and forever be with you, wishing that it were you who was lying beside me.

He Isn't The One

His kisses leave me parched,
For he doesn't quench my thirst.
His touch leaves me cold,
For he doesn't fuel my fire.
His love leaves me starved,
For he doesn't feed my hunger.

He isn't the one I love,
Only the man I'm lying next to.

The One

Considering that I have loved you since the very beginning, I would just simply assume that you would be more considerate instead of so self-indulged; that you would care just a little bit more.

I would move all of the mountains that stood tall in our way. I would destroy every living creature that fell within our path.

I needed you to function, to breathe for me even only half as much as I did for you.

Our history was too strong; we had been through entirely too much to not love each other fully.

But you—

You were incapable of loving anything fully, beside yourself.

He Wanted

He wanted me to dress the way he said,
Speak the way he liked,
Love the way he couldn't,
Do all of the things he wouldn't,
And I always did everything he asked.
I did it for him.

My Drug

I realize now that I had been lying when I told people I never touched a drug before,
Because just one touch, one tiny taste of you and it was never enough—
Somehow, I was always left needing more.
You were always my only addiction,
You were my drug of choice.

Breathe

"That boy, he is in love with you." My mother so confidently told me.

"How do you know?"

"Oh darling, it's in the way he can't catch his breath whenever he looks at you."

I was also having quite some trouble breathing.

How He Adored Her

He adored her.

When he looked at her, there was no questioning his feelings at all; everyone already knew, and could see the way his lovesick eyes would flicker as she smiled.

He was simply consumed, and remembered every single detail that consisted of her,

Like how the first time he ever laid eyes on her was on a Monday, but the first words they ever shared were the following Friday.

He knew *everything* about her,

From what made her heart flutter, to what made her mind tick. He noticed how many times she pulled down her dress as it rode up her thigh, to the exact science she had while she strutted in her heels.

He constantly imagined her in her natural habitat—in front of a roaring fire curled up with a good book and a fresh mug of herbal tea; a picture she painted for him a million times.

He knew that her favorite desert was coconut almond cake dressed with vanilla icing and that she could only handle one glass of Moscato before the wine spilled through her veins and began to take over her body.

He loved how she tasted of confusion and wore the scent of summer.

He admired how she saw such significant importance in goodbyes.

She was his inspiration, and all he ever wanted was to be drunk within her presence.

Incompatible

We still care deeply for each other till this very day—
We will forever have a love that no outside soul will
understand,
But we will only admire each other from a distance
Because we are just incompatible; I was too structured and
he, too wild
And although we would have given our last dying breath for
the other, it was irrelevant.
Once we loved each other so fully,
And lost each other so tragically;
We were opposites,
Like the sun and the moon—
We could not coexist together.

That Look

That look he gives me—
The look of admiration,
It makes me want him even more than I ever thought possible.
I just desperately wish I knew exactly what was going on in his head while he's admiring me from afar—
All of the things he wants to say, but is too afraid to speak out loud into existence.
Sometimes I think he's looking at me like he'll never see me again…
Like he knows something I don't.
But what do I know?
I am constantly over thinking and over analyzing.

In The Night

Owls always instilled fear in me.
They are patient creatures
Waiting all day only to make their appearance during the darkest hours.
They choose their victims wisely,
Slowly hunting, then takes them down when they least expect it,
Never to be seen until it is too late.
This is what you did to me.
You were the owl, and I the defenseless prey; thinking the coast was clear, only to be torn apart.

Everywhere

How can I move on when I live my life being so consumed of him? I live each day anticipating his arrival, seeing his face, and feeling his hands on my skin again.

How can I move on when I see him everywhere?

I see him when I'm blinded by the sun and redirected by the moon.

I see him in the inconsistent beauty of the waves crashing against the shoreline.

I see him in every romance movie I watch, every love story I read.

I see him and I slow dancing, as he holds me close.

I see him at the receiving end as I walk down the isle.

I see him playing catch at the park with our children, patiently waiting to be born.

All roads, they always lead me straight back to him.

Awake

I wondered if I would ever sleep again,
If there would be a time when I would gracefully drift off all
the way through the night.
If there would be a moment he wouldn't captivate all of my
thoughts, both as I lay awake, and finally unconscious once
sleep takes over my mind.
I wondered, would there be a single night I wouldn't dream
of him?
A new day I would wake up not wanting him?
A morning I wouldn't be utterly disappointed by the
emptiness of my blank white walls being my first sight as I
open my eyes, instead of his beautiful eyes and perfect full
lips?
All I knew was that I still craved him.
I still needed him the same way I needed to consume water,
Or the way I needed to breathe in oxygen.
I could feel myself slipping away, for I was only fueling my
body with things that consisted of him.
But he was poison, you see
And he was slowly killing me.
I was actually dying for him,
Simply because he had stopped living for me;
And I was doing everything to still feel him,
Anything, to keep his presence alive.

All I Wanted

I wanted to be with the man, who knew me,
Who knew how I took my coffee,
Who knew the tears behind my eyes,
Who knew how to catch them once they began to fall.
The man who would make me want to dance, regardless of how I couldn't.
The man who would kiss me without being asked, simply because he would always crave the taste of my lips,
The man who remembers every single detail from every single interaction we ever shared
Like what I was wearing,
How I was sitting,
The way my hair fell in front of my face,
Or what my smile did to his soul once his eyes first lay upon it.

The Way We Happened

I'm glad that we happened in the way that we did.
We found each other during a time of desperation.
We leaned on each other when we lost all else.
We became so hypnotized, so infected with one another that
we became diseased.
I now know that we weren't meant to be,
Or maybe our timing was just wrong.
We were on different ends of the spectrum; I was the sun
and he the moon.
So you see, we never really stood a chance, for the odds were
always against us.

Saving Grace

I racked my brain for months that felt like lifetimes trying to figure out what was wrong with me, trying desperately to understand why *I* wasn't enough to change him.

But then I realized,

You can never be enough to the man who will never be ready.

This doesn't mean you aren't good enough; it means *he* isn't.

This doesn't mean you are not worth his love; it means *he* isn't worthy of yours.

But he was aware of this long before I, and that was the only saving grace—
He allowed me to leave
Once he realized he would never be able to be become a better man
For himself,
And for me.

All Of Him

I only ever wanted to be completely consumed in him.
I wanted to swim in his mind, and drown in his thoughts.
To find true genuine substance within his words,
To hear his passions, hopes, dreams, and deepest fears.
I wanted simplicity within connection, not in conversation.
I wanted to know what kept him awake at night, what motivated him to continue on each day.
I wanted to carefully pick apart his soul piece by piece and unravel the bandages that were protecting his old wounds made by the ghosts of his past.
I wanted to know why he was so protective over his heart, and why he liked to hide away from the rest of the universe.
I just wanted to know him in every last way that I could,
But he never really let me all the way in.
I only ever got glimpses of his soul, but was never really immersed in it.
He was like that; keeping the world at arm's length, preventing pain any way he could.
But I wanted him to know that I wouldn't hurt him.
I wanted him to know that I would protect him,
That I would never walk out or leave his side,
That I would cut myself before I'd ever consider holding the blade to his skin.
I just wanted to be suffocated by all things that were him.

Tricks

My mind plays tricks on me in the dark of the night.
It makes me remember
All the things I have desperately been attempting to forget.
I begin to miss you,
And all that we once were;
Thinking back on all the things that were you, that were us.
Haunted by memories of a life that existed long ago,
In another lifetime, perhaps.
We are nothing more than people who didn't know that they
were meant to live their lives as strangers, never actually
destined to interject.

Timeless

He was only mine for a moment etched in time, but I would take that tiny moment over a hundred lifetimes with any other soul.

Our love, it was a timeless classic; forever destined to stay in style.

She Wanted

She wanted her heart to feel again,
She wanted her heart to heal again,
But each time a heart is broken, it is never really put back
together the same way it was once before.

Heartbreak

Someone once asked me how to get over heartbreak. I couldn't respond, because I didn't know how. The truth is, that after all of this time, I am still very much living in it. The truth is, that till this very day, I still feel the pain in my heart and that sharpness in my gut only when I think of him; when I am surrounded by things that remind me of him Like when I hear his favorite song on the radio, Spot a Snickers bar at the checkout counter, Or loose my mind to the loneliness that creeps in at 4A.M. I don't think you ever get over heartbreak. You simply learn to live with it, with your heart forever being slightly damaged and never completely full again.

Day 184

Day 184—3:14A.M.,
Unable to sleep.
I cannot begin to breathe or catch my breath
Frantic, while thoughts of you continue to consume me.

It is on day 184—
184 days without your lips on mine,
Without your warm touch,
Your gentle voice,
And your endearing eyes memorizing mine
That I realize
There is no remedy for a broken heart.

184 days deep,
And it is as though it were day one all over again,
For I can still feel my heart shattering into mere pieces
That may one day be picked up off the ground—
But can only be pieced imperfectly back together.
My heart can never again be the way it once was
Before you.

I Wonder

I wonder,
If you know that you hold such a prominent space in the depth of my mind,
A special home I have placed aside just for you.
I wonder,
If you still think about me, as much as I do you.
Do you still worry about me, though I am not near?
Do you hope that I cut down on all that damn coffee my body had grown so dependent on?
Do you question if my heart still belongs to you,
Or think about the tragic possibility of me being secure within another's hold?
Does your heart still stop when someone speaks my name?
Does your skin still crawl when someone else's fingertips grace your skin?
Do you still pray for me before you rest your eyes each night?
Do you still struggle not to write me each morning as you wake?

I just wonder—
Do I still cross your mind?

Johnny Depp

He reminded me of a young Johnny Depp, and who doesn't love a pretty boy with a little bit of rock and roll flowing through his veins?

He was a little rough around the edges, but I could still feel the sweetness pouring out of him.

He lived in V-necks and black leather jackets,

He had cheekbones that could cut glass,

Sensual brown eyes I would loose myself in,

Lips that I had grown addicted to kissing…

The softest hair my fingers had ever graced,

And a collarbone that housed thousands of kisses my lips left behind.

He had this soul that was so wild, there was no cage built strong enough to tame it,

And an attitude that was so bad, it was actually the sweetest thing I ever tasted.

Bartenders And Musicians

My momma always told me to stay away from bartenders
and musicians,
So it's ironic that he was a little bit of both.
He mixed the best drinks to get me drunk, so I would
incoherently spill all of the secrets my soul was keeping.
He learned the perfect note to my heart, and played that
chord so beautifully that I couldn't even be mad at him when
he went on to break it later.

Essence

There is something in the essence of his soul that I will always be drawn to,
Like a helpless moth to a deadly flame.
Maybe it was the way he made any words scripted on paper sound like a symphony once spoken out loud,
Or the way he tasted my tears as they slid down my skin.
It could have even been the way his face melted into my hand as my fingers wiped away the lipstick stain I had left behind.
It was as though he had been written in a completely different language, that I fiercely studied, but never did fully understand.

The Way We Were

I watched *The Way We Were* again tonight,
And although I have seen this classic film hundreds of times,
it struck a different chord in my heart this late November
evening
As tears continued to stain my cheeks,
For it was the first time I have watched this film since
meeting you,
Since loving you,
And then ultimately loosing you.
I was hit with the tragic reminder of us,
Of how our love, yet beautiful, was simply not enough.

Our love, like so many others, could not conquer all.

Cancer

I was never a believer in astrology,
However, his zodiac sign suited him perfectly,
For he was a cancer in every humanly way possible;
Complete poison for my entire body,
And no matter how many treatments I endured,
He always seemed to spread.
I was never able to rid myself of the cancer that was he.

I Saved Everything

I saved everything that ever came from you,
From every insignificant message you ever sent,
To every voicemail you ever left.
I even saved the wrapper from the very first candy you ever
gave me.
I read your messages from time to time,
Just to relive a moment when you loved me—
To remember that it was real,
And didn't live only in my imagination.
They ask me, "Why hold on to something he threw away
so long ago?"

To remember all the magic we made,
To remind myself
That your love,
Was worth all the tragic pain.

Why

I had a million questions that needed answers
But the only one worth asking was why...
Why didn't you trust yourself enough to love me?

Endearing

It was actually endearing
The way he looked at me with such pain behind his eyes,
Like he was doing everything possible with his own two
beautiful hands not to hurt me.
But I was too fragile, and his touch was just too rough.
I now believe it was simply in my fate, to become broken
only by him.

Saved

She was always trying to save everyone.

She thought that she could fix them, all those druggies and misfits.

Maybe, if she had given enough of herself to their troubled souls, it could be enough.

Maybe, she thought, just maybe if she loved the unloved, she could fix the unfixable.

"You're not helping them," he finally informed her. "You've only become another addiction."

Untouched

"I always thought I wanted a girl as pure and untouched as she was
Until I finally had the chance to claim her, and realized that I didn't deserve her.
A rarity such as her deserved not only the moon, but also every shooting star in the galaxy, when all I could offer her was the black hole where my heart once lived.
There was a slight possibility that she could fill it up again, make me whole again,
Or I would completely suck her in, forever damaging her, stripping her of her pureness,
And that was a risk I simply was not willing to take."

Cry

Sometimes you need to cry.
You just do.
You need to feel the tears fall down your cheek and stain your skin.
I swear, there were moments I cried so hard I believed I would drown in my own tears—
Moments that I could actually feel the pain exciting my body, the way demons are rejected from a possessed human soul,
And every single time I felt reborn.

He Wasn't Mine

I think I became so obsessive,
So territorial, l strictly because I never actually had him—
He was never really mine to begin with,
And that is where the infatuation struck,
The pride took over,
And the lust got confused with love.

Measure Of Love

We should measure our love not by what we have,
But by what we have to offer.

We should measure our love not by what has been *given to*
us,
But by what has been *given up* by us.

You see, love is all about sacrifice.
If we never sacrifice,
Then we never really learn how to love—
We'll only know how to accept it,
And this is a tragedy all in itself,
Because the biggest gift one can offer
Is their unconditional love.

Anchor

I had a dream that I was drowning.
Time after time my fingers would almost pierce through the surface,
But then the tide would suck me back under.
Further I would fall into the ocean's dark abyss
As the anchor, that is you, continued to hold me hostage.
I grasped as the water filled my lungs, furiously and all at once.
I awoke with my heart pounding and mind racing.
It was here, in the middle of the night, awoken from this treacherous nightmare,
That I realized if I continued to hold onto you,
You would continue to suck me down.
I need to cut my ties,
To release my anchor that is you.
I have to reach the surface and feel the sun on my face,
I just need to breathe once again,
To loose the weight of this anchor, and survive.

Always Loosing

I am always losing when it comes to you,
For when I am not with you, it feels like I am suffocating,
unable to catch my breath
And when I am with you, I am constantly drowning deep
within your presence.
I simply cannot win.

Over Thinking

He told me to stop over thinking,
But how can I not always over analyze when he is always
leaving?

My Truth

My truth,
Is that you are the only heartbreak my body has ever known.

My heart still cries out to you, even through the silence of my pursed lips.

I haven't stopped searching for your face in every crowd, down every street and every lane.

My truth,
Is that after all of this time, I am still secretly praying that God will bring us back together again, some day.

My Mind Plays Tricks

I should only go by what I see,
And what I see is that you have moved on
Seeking the attention of anyone who will give it.
My eyes tell me that I am no longer the one putting the smile
on your face,
Or the protectiveness in your nature.
You no longer look for the comfort I once offered.

But I am programmed differently,
For I only know to go by what I feel,
And what I feel is still so connected to you—
That your behavior is only in defense,
For your pain and your grief;
That your brain is trying to convince you to move on,
But your heart and your soul simply will not allow it.
They are on my side, and they are fighting for us.
You still care. I know that you do, I can feel it even in the
depths of my pores...

Is my mind playing tricks on me?
Probably.

Everlasting

The waves will crash against the shoreline and wash away every love note ever written in the sand.
The rain will fall upon every broken soul and clean them of their sins.
Our footsteps placed in the soil will be wiped away with the years to come and
One day this world may destroy every thing that we have ever known,

But my love for you will be everlasting.

I wanted his ugly before his beautiful,
Disaster before magic,
Authenticity and passion; not structure and balance.

But he only wanted me to paint a pretty picture; he never
craved my truth.

I wanted him in his rawest form.
He wanted me on my best behavior.

All We Will Never Be

After all the time that has passed,
Even until this very day,
It is still hard to be in the same room as you
And be reminded
Of all of the things we couldn't overcome,
All the things we will never get the chance to be.

Old Friend

Hello old friend.
It is so bittersweet to see you after all of this time,
A meeting I have been mentally preparing for.
Not much has changed,
Yet everything has.
You still wear that same boyish grin
As you sip your corona.
That same sexual tension is in the air, and it can be cut with
the dullest knife.
Don't worry; I will be on my best behavior, for I know she
is not far away.

You cannot help but to pull me in just a bit closer,
Same as it only comes natural holding your face in my hand.
Does she know that you still struggle with staying faithful?
Has she seen how aggressive you can be when things don't
go your way?
Does she give you space and allow you to seek out her?
Does she know that for a long time you were the only thing
I could think about?
That you were the only form of consistency I knew?
Does she know about me?
About how beautiful we were together?

I hope she is not mad as my fingers grace your arm,
Or the way your hand wanders down my back.

My God, I have never been this close to your lips without
kissing them.

It is taking everything in me,
But I promise, I will restrain.

Clumsy

I have always been clumsy,
So when I naturally stumbled into you
I didn't see it as destiny,
Just another unfortunate fall.

He Asked Me

"Does it still hurt you to look at me?"

"Considering that looking at you is a constant reminder of *almost* holding in my hand everything I thought I ever wanted; only to lose it all without any say, any control... it was like living in the perfect picture—a Norman Rockwell painting, only to have a tornado come and destroy it all— every home, every dream we were building together... Your potential is outstanding, yet you choose to settle for a life of passionless mediocrity. So honestly? Yeah, *It fucking kills me.*"

Dig

I wanted him to fall in love with my mind the same way I had fallen in love with his.
But he liked what he saw on the outside,
So he felt no need to dig through my pretty little head.
It was always easier for me, to grab my shovel and dig incredibly far too deep beyond the surface,
Too deep for my own good.

Wasn't Me

It wasn't me. I know that now.
It took me a while, but better late than never, right?
Like I've written hundreds of times,
On hundreds of different pages,
I wanted to fix what seemed to be broken.
But he was born with venom in his veins,
And I came entirely too late to suck it out.
He will forever be a self-righteous narcissist, who will only
know how to love himself.

So why am I still praying he will walk through that door?

Withdrawals

I swear, I thought I was in control of my cravings.
I hadn't realized that I became addicted,
Until my body endured such awful withdrawals
As your poison escaped me veins.

Your Tainted Love

And in an instant,
I would take your tainted loved
From your damaged heart
Over any complete love
Another could offer.

Crown

So finally I will lay my crown down at your feet.
I was never your princess,
I only pretended to be.

Naked

Naked with every thought exposed,
Ease into my conscious.
Be gentle while you tare me apart in your most gracious
way possible.
Take me.
I am yours for the keeping.

Lips

Shame on me
To just simply assume,
That those lips aren't being kissed by another,
That after all of this time,
Your lips
Still belong to mine.

He

He had many admirers, more than most.
He couldn't walk into a room without every ounce of attention on him,
All eyes stuck to him like glue.
Not only because he was beautiful beyond comprehension,
But because he had something inside of him that flowed from his eyes
And instantly captured everyone's hearts.
It was almost as though you could feel his soul spilling from his pores.
I swear to you, I could actually touch his goodness when I looked into his eyes.

Bees

Like a bear to honey I was sticking to you,
But you weren't quite ready
And I was stung while trying to claim you.
It was then, that I learned I'm allergic to bees.

Wasn't Enough

I began to walk away feeling slighted, defeated.

"*Riss,*" I always fell a little more in love when his tender voice spoke the nickname he appointed.

I turned to face him.

"You know I love you."

All I could say in response was the truth.

"You know I wish that were enough."

In that moment I wanted to take all of his self-inflicted hate away.

I wanted to take his pain and make it my own.

I walked two steps toward him, held his gorgeous face in my hand, and kissed his cheek one last time.

"I love you too." I whispered so tightly into his ear as the words fell from my lips.

I wanted to ensure only his soul will feel these words, but the universe will never meet them.

In one motion, I turned to walk away.

I couldn't look at him, so I locked into the cold pavement instead, as the concrete became one with my tears once they started to fall.

Brighter Than The Sun

I loved him in a way that the earth was jealous—
Jealous, because my love shined upon him brighter than
The sun's rays could ever shine upon this earth.

Trust

I am learning to trust in the process of this life.
I am learning to believe that life always has way of working
out,
That everything will happen the way it is supposed to.

What is meant for me will always be mine—
I will not have to fight for it,
Nor share it.
I will let things come,
And allow them to go.

I am sick of fighting for what wasn't meant to stay.
I am tired of holding on to things that have already served
their purpose.
I am over trying to play God.

Back To Him

"Would you go back to something that you already knew?"
He asked me.

It was then, that he looked through my eyes, and my soul
gave away the answer before any words could leave my lips.

"Yes my love. I will always come right back to you."

NYE

As the ball dropped, he found me.
He kissed my cheek and held me tight.
His lips, they missed mine,
But we had come too far to go back to what we were before.
"I love you baby girl." He whispered as his lips left my skin.
"Be safe" was all I knew to respond.

"Be safe" with her heart—safer than you were with mine...

And So I Ran

I was always either running late,
Running away,
Or running out of time.

Our Soul

And when he left, I felt my entire life falling into pieces, like the world was ending and beautiful skyscrapers were tumbling to the ground, becoming mere rubble

Simply because

My soul,
His soul,
Our soul,

It was one—
And because of this, I simply could not exist with half of me missing.

Fate

I was messing with our fate—
Fighting to hold on to him.
The truth is,
He was never mine to keep.

3:35 a.m.

His soul—
It was tied to mine now
And there was no escaping that tragic law.

And because he is now apart of me
I know
The same way I am now,
He is also awake out there
Somewhere
Unable to sleep—
Because he is thinking about me too.

He Used To

He used to look at me like I was the only living thing in the galaxy—
Like he had just discovered life on a new planet.

If My Writing Brought Him Back

I used to think that writing would bring him back to me—
That's why I allowed myself to drown in my own words.
But instead, it only made me realize how distant he had in
fact become.

Pretty Lies

I wasn't in my right mind when I told you that I loved you,
For I was blinded by a pretty face that spoke even prettier
lies.

Trust In God

The bible says, "For I know the plans *I have for you*," Declares the Lord, "Plans to prosper you and not to harm you, plans to *give you hope and a future*." Jeremiah 29:11

My future, I saw him. I always saw him.
But God, he had different plans.
You see, I tried to be in control for far too long.
I tried to make my future strictly what I wanted it be to.
I was playing God instead of trusting in him.
And that was my downfall.

Settle

What a terribly tragic realization
To know that there are people in this world
Who will spend the rest of their lives
Laying next to someone,
While still dreaming of another.

Pieces Of Me

There are pieces of me still in him—
Silly girl, why are you settling for the broken fragments I
have left behind?
You know that when he's looking at you
He's only wishing
You were I.

He Wanted A Lie

And when she got her dream boy
She lost him, quickly,
Because the dream boy asked his dream girl for the fantasy—
He never wanted reality.

I Was Different

I was different to him.
He was incredibly smooth,
Charming,
Surprisingly thoughtful,
And even more surprisingly caring.
I didn't know if it was me who struck his heart to feel something magical
Or if it was an act—this was all part of his vindictive little game.
But I did get my validation—
"We've never seen him like this before. He must be *falling in love with you.*"

But it didn't matter.
I had arrived too late.
I still wasn't enough to change him.

Change

When I was younger, I believed with my whole heart that people have the ability to change.
I swore that if someone, no matter how far gone or damaged they seem to be, if they found that spark, that being for their sole existence, then they would be better.

How naïve of me to think that someone could change the core of whom they are, despite how ugly.

It wasn't until I met him, that everything altered.
He gave me a passion that I had never endured.
He showed me a love that I never knew.

But the thing is this; by the time I found him, it was too late to change him;
He was, in fact, too far gone.
I wanted to make him better, strictly because *he deserved* to be better.
But sometimes, people just are who they are.
They reach an age where they are no longer impressionable;
The way you find them is the only way you get to keep them.

This doesn't mean that they don't love you; this just means that they spent their whole lives loving themselves more, and now, they simply don't know any better.

Blind

I never believed them when they said love is blind,
Until I ran head first into you.
For when it came to you
I only saw what I wanted to see,
Yet my vision was blurred to everything I didn't.

Tortured

By memories I can't escape—
Haunted by promises he couldn't keep.

Don't Ask Me

Don't ask me why I love him,
For I know he is not worthy.
Don't ask me why I still pray for him,
For I already know his soul is damned.
Don't ask me why I still write to him,
For I know he will never read these words.
Don't ask me why I still cry out to him,
For I know he has become deaf to my voice.
Don't ask me why he still holds my heart,
For I know his belongs to another.

Pride

Anyone with vision could see the way they felt for each other,
Even though they always refused to admit it.

It was in the way she never failed to make him smile, no
matter the weight his shoulders were carrying.

Or the way she could never bring herself to stay mad at him,
even though she had been the queen of holding grudges.

It was whenever he spoke of her; he couldn't control his
endearment,
And when she would see him, her eyes would start to sparkle
like diamonds.
When he heard her voice, his eyes danced around the room
until he spotted her,
And when he spoke her name, her heart skipped a beat.

And the sad truth
Is that they never actually allowed themselves to love each
other the way they could have,
Simply because they were too proud,
And they made their pride more important
Than their love should have been.

Easy

To love is all too easy.

Falling in love with him came so effortlessly.
It was committing to each other that was entirely harder
than expected.
It was then, that I realized how most things in life are
actually incredibly simple.
The problem is us; we make them much more complicated
than they need to be.

My Name

I fell in love with the way he said my name,
The way he held my fragile heart in the palm of his hand,
And that one look that had the power to make me forget all
the sinful harm he had caused me.

Quicksand

I stood steadily, both feet planted securely on the ground.
But loose ends reopened got the best of me
And like quicksand, the ground beneath my feet sucked me down,
And suffocated me under the surface of his words.

Storms

There is a storm in my soul that is out of control.
There are waves crashing against my rib cage.
My lungs are drowning in the chaos that echoes through my veins.
This only occurs when he absent from my flesh—
But once I find him, he is always the only cure to calm my storms.

Talk Less, Listen More

We all want to surround ourselves with people
Who talk a little less
And listen a little more.

So shouldn't we be carrying the same characteristics we
seek in others?

Exclusive Soul

They only care when it is convenient—
So do me a favor,
And don't ever let them take you for granted.
They always prey on the ones with the beautiful hearts and
passionate souls;
For they are forever forgiving
And always dependable.
So listen to me when I tell you—
It is okay to be picky with who you let in.
Not everyone deserves to know your soul.

Please only allow your soul to be exclusive for the few worthy
ones.

Thoughtful

Out of everything I could have been in the world, all I really wanted was to be thoughtful.
To be unapologetically aware of everyone else.
I wanted to be someone who remembered details—
All of the little fragments of instances that made moments come together,
That made them beautiful beyond comprehension.
To remember all the little things onlookers found so easy to forget.
Someone who knew the remedy to turning a bad day into a good one,
With encouraging words of hope
Or a kind gesture.
I wanted to be the person that *I* needed when times got tough, the person that I never had.
This world needs more of that.
Yeah. I wanted to be that for someone.

He'll Come

He will come knocking with promises and arms filled with hope.
He will always have the right words to say.
He'll tell you he cares, and you'll always believe him.

But don't get used to his sweet gestures.
He isn't a gentleman, he's only pretending.
He'll stop going out of his way once his selfish needs overpower him.
He can hide his truth for a little while,
But true colors always bleed through the surface.

So always wear your armor—
For he will be the killer of your heart
And destruction of your soul.

Two Lovers

Her heart was torn between two lovers:
The man saturated in grace as he planted soft kisses gently
upon her fragile skin each morning,
And the monster that emerged once the whisky emptied
every night.

Forgive Me

I thought of you today
And began to cry, uncontrollably.
I loved you so much that I swore I could change you

But my love, it just wasn't enough.

I feel like I failed you.

I know that it isn't my fault—
Yet I can't bring myself to blame you.

I am so sorry that I wasn't able to heal you.

Please
Forgive me.

And like a heartbeat,
He kept me alive.

Bad With Goodbyes

"I was bad with goodbyes
That's why we never had one.
I just couldn't bring myself to say goodbye to her,
Well not officially that is
Because saying goodbye to her was saying goodbye to everything I had ever known, everything I had ever loved.

The last time I saw her will forever be etched into my memory.
It was a Sunday night; the summer weather had already faded into the late September air, fall beginning to take over.
She was getting ready to leave me after spending the day together.
I watched her for a few moments as she fiddled around and gathered her things.
I was taking it all in, the way she tucked a strand of her soft hair behind her pretty little ear, the way she wrinkled her nose and the flustered look on her face, making sure she wasn't forgetting anything.
I made sure to take a mental picture of her flawless face so I would never forget a single feature: the beauty mark just above her upper lip, the dimples on either side of her cheeks that only made an appearance when she smiled fully, her big brown doe eyes. I could never help myself from getting lost in them...

I hadn't even realized I was staring until her voice came into focus. She was wondering why I was staring at her the way that I was.

She didn't realize I was simply admiring her one last time.

I had always adored her, and sometimes was so obvious about it a blind man would be able to see the way she made me smile.

I constantly found myself being struck with awe when I would look at her, when I would watch her in all she would do—
The way she moved,
The concentration on her face as she read a book that enthralled her,
How easily distracted she became whenever I'd walk into a room.

She walked over to me arms wide open, smile planted upon her face.

I opened my arms to her and held her as I continued to take in every single last detail.

I memorized the way her small frame fit perfectly within my hold as I breathed her in one last time.

"Where's my kiss?" she said smiling as she pointed to her cheek.

I grabbed her face and kissed her, I was grateful I got to feel my lips on her porcelain skin one last time.

She smiled, turned and walked away.

"I'll see ya later handsome."

I swallowed her words as she spoke them.

I was hypnotized by her angelic voice, and at the same time tormented by the fact that this would be the last time I would hear it.

I said nothing, but was mesmerized as I watched her walk away and walk out of my life.

She wouldn't see me again. This was our final goodbye and she didn't even know it.

They would say I was selfish, not allowing her to have the proper goodbye she would have wanted, especially since they were so important to her. They would say it wasn't fair, that I was able to mentally prepare myself to be without her, that I was able to take it all in and leave her with just a distant memory and a million questions and too many why's.

They would call me selfish, but they couldn't be more wrong. *I saved her from all the pain.*

Goodbyes, they are entirely too hard, incredibly too painful. I saved her from all that.

I was the one who was hurting.

I was the one who had to live with the knowledge that I would never be in her presence again; that when enough time passes she will be able to forget me, but I–

I will forever be searching for her face everywhere I go in hopes that maybe, just maybe I can catch one more glimpse of her smile, or hear one more flicker of her laughter.

But I know better.

I will always know better, and isn't that the worst part of it all?

That I will forever be tortured with the truth of not being able to get lost in those eyes again?

I would rather be in her position, living in the unknown.

Besides, I think this is my saving grace, the only good thing I have left–

Leaving her alone and allowing her to move on once I realized that she was too good for me. I could never be enough for her. She is an angel full of grace and beauty, and I a mere mortal, filled with nothing but sin and destruction. I could never be more than that. I wasn't worthy of her love.

Trust me when I tell you, **I did save her,** but I know she wouldn't see it that way.
I know her though, and I know this was easier.
This was the only way to let her move on.
I hope she can forgive me."

Him

I would be lying if I said I first fell for his character over his perfect features.

He was, by far, the most beautiful man I had ever seen in my entire life. So yes, the fact that he was drop dead gorgeous was obviously my first thought when I laid eyes on him. My second thought: trouble.

Did I judge him? Yes. I hate that I did. But, I hate even more that my judgment didn't fail me. He was trouble. He told me so himself. It was a Saturday night once the summer sun had fallen and the moon took its place. It was then, that night in-between passionate kisses and wandering hands under the stars when he warned me.

"I'm scared of you" he informed me, *"scared of not being enough for you."*
"I DON'T WANT TO RUIN THIS."

We were both falling far too deep. It's funny you know, I don't think either one of us expected these feelings to so seamlessly emerge as they did. But it happened. Our soul's fell in love too quickly to keep up. We couldn't control it. We tried, but we couldn't stop it. So, we just went with it.

For the first time in his life, he actually tried. For the first time, he was able to feel something genuine and put another soul before his own. He met me, and he began to question his existence.

He told me he valued me for the woman I was, for the morals and lifestyle I had chosen to live.

He respected me for both the purity of my heart, and body. He was, for the first time, confronted with a task he couldn't overcome, a woman who will never fully subject herself to him.

Placed right in the palm of his hand was what he was so desperately missing all of these years. All he had to do was lace his fingers around me, and I would be his own. You see, his excuse for all of this time was that his love just wasn't out there. There were no good girls left, for I did not exist. So once his dream girl finally found him, he was forced to face the true issue, which was HE. He wasn't ready. He was never going to be ready. He was simply too used to the life he had been living, and didn't know anything else. He was too old to change, too set in his ways.

We both wanted more. We both needed more. But he would never be able to give me what I needed, which was all of him. I wanted his heart mind and soul to belong only to me. I couldn't bear to share this man, but he didn't know how to belong to a single woman. He didn't know how not to be selfish.

This didn't make him a bad person; in fact, his enchanting soul matched his radiant exterior. But, by the time I found him, he had already passed the point of no return. It was a constant struggle, to sit back and watch a man I immensely cared for just settle for a life he didn't want. He had all this potential that he was incapable of reaching.

So, we just couldn't work. Sometimes, love, simply is not enough.

I will never forget him. He will always be apart of me. He had become a piece of my identity in the same way my own name was. I think that's what happens to the ones we've loved and lost, the ones that truly mattered and impacted our lives; they become branded in us. And I believe that we never fully forget; that hole in our hearts that have been created in their absence never really gets filled back in all of the way, we just simply learn to live without them. They will forever have a piece of our unconscious thoughts. But I do believe that as time passes and we continue to age, the pain will begin to fade. We will be able to look back and remember them through a pure smile, and there is beauty within this thought alone.

Sometimes it is hard for me to make sense of us. I like to believe that things happen for a reason, and that we happened for a reason. It's better than thinking we were only meant to admire each other from a safe distance, anyway. Truth be told, I didn't know how to stay away from a man I shared such an unexplainable chemistry with just from the very first glance. When we first locked eyes, the connection was instantaneous, effortless. I was tied to him from the very beginning, like I had always known him. So I don't know what's right from wrong. I don't know if I was supposed to keep him at arms length, or if he *was* meant to be the huge force in my life he became. I guess I just have to settle with the simple thought that people enter our worlds and leave for our own lessons, and just be okay with that.

Maybe we didn't end up having a happily ever after but that's okay. What we had, it was special. It was beautiful and no one can take that away.

He cared for me to the very best of his ability. He cared about me as much as his heart allowed him to be capable, and I must be able to take comfort in that alone.

He will forever have a piece of my soul. He will forever flow through my pores and run through my veins. I have undoubting faith that I will find absolute happiness within another, and when I do find the man who will know how to love me the way I need, the way I deserve, I promise that by then I would have stopped living for *him*, but I will never be able to bring myself to completely stop loving *him*.

Know This

I do not know everything,
But I do know this—
That tomorrow
The sun will rise at dawn,
And set once again at dusk.
The moon will appear in its place,
And the North Star will guide you home.
Love will always enter your life.
If you are lucky it will stay,
But sometimes it will go,
Regardless it will always come back to you.
If you are broken tonight,
You have the chance to be repaired tomorrow.
If you feel empty right now,
You will feel full again.
Give this life of yours some time.
I promise,
You will always be okay again.

Closing

I was never one for letting go. I, like so many people, feel everything very deeply and hold on to things even when I can actually feel them sucking the life out of me. I keep them bottled up deep inside and consume me in every humanly destructive way possible. I've been guilty of holding onto grudges, toxic people and memories that do nothing but bring me pain. But know this, writing has healed my heart every single time it was broken. Writing has become my only gateway to sanity, and for that I am forever grateful. Find your gateway. Through prayer and God I have been able to find comfort and peace. Once you learn to let go, you will be able to heal. LEARN TO LET GO. It is the only way you will survive

People do not get the privilege to tell you not to hurt. They don't get to tell you not to feel pain and they most certainly don't get to tell you how to love. Follow, but most importantly, PROTECT your heart always, for it is the most honest, purest thing you hold in your possession.
"Above all else, guard your heart, for everything you do flows from it." Proverbs 4:23

I do not have all of the answers, and I am still learning as I go, but if you take one thing with you, please learn how to simply enjoy the little moments in life that make your heart feel something beautiful.

I want to thank you, with everything inside of me, thank you for taking this journey with me.

With love,
Marisa